Mel Bay Presen

Contra Dance
ENCYCLOPEDIA

MW00913836

by John Holenko

2 3 4 5 6 7 8 9 0

Visit us on the Web at www.melbay.com — E-mail us at email@melbay.com

Contents

John Holenko

John Holenko has performed on classical guitar, steel-string guitar, mandolin, banjo and historic instruments throughout the United States and in Europe. Called "a skilled soloist" by the Boston Globe, Mr. Holenko has given recitals and been featured in radio broadcasts in New York, Los Angeles, Boston, and San Francisco. As a member of the early music ensemble Sonus, Mr. Holenko has performed on historic instruments in recitals here in the United States and in Europe.

John Holenko performs on mandolin and steel-string guitar with his group The Hungry Monks, an eclectic, acoustic ensemble playing a wide variety of traditional and original music.

John Holenko has been on the faculty of Charleston Southern University and The College of Charleston. He is also the Guitarist, Mandolinist, and Banjo player for the Charleston Symphony Orchestra. Mr. Holenko is very active in music education through his own private studio, Hungry Monk Music, and residencies through the South Carolina Arts Commission. John has been an instructor in music at the Charlotte Children's Theatre in Charlotte, NC, and at the Cuyahoga Valley Environmental Education Center in Ohio, where he has also been Artist-in Residence.

Mel Bay Publications has published editions of Medieval music and Renaissance music for mandolin by Mr. Holenko.

John Holenko received degrees in Classical Guitar performance from the New England Conservatory, and the University of Southern California, also studying historic performance at both institutions, and premiering many new works.

I. Introduction to the music

In the early 1990's, a group of musician's in Charleston, SC began to perform traditional American and Celtic dance tunes for the contra dance community there. Eventually this group coalesced into The Donnybrook Legacy. While also performing in concert settings and for private functions, The Donnybrook Legacy remained primarily a Contra dance band and built it's repertoire around those needs. Eventually, the group broke up into several different bands, all of whom continue to play for dances in Charleston and throughout the Southeast. Our current band, The Hungry Monks, uses much of the material developed by The Donnybrook while adding a whole bunch more tunes and sets.

This book presents much of the material used by these groups for contra dancing. In an effort to present our material the way we would perform it, we have arranged the dances into sets of two or more tunes, just as we put them together for a dance. All these tunes fit into three categories: reels, jigs, and waltzes. The reels and jigs are put together into sets for contra dances, while the waltzes stand alone. While we find that these sets work well both for the dancers as well as musically by themselves, these are just suggestions. You will also find a section of Reels and Jigs that are not grouped together. You should feel free to substitute any of these into our sets, add to our sets with any of these tunes, or make up your own sets using these tunes. You are encouraged to mix and match as you see fit, and of course add to this collection with your own favorite tunes

II. What is Contra Dancing?

Contra Dancing, also known as Old-Time Contra Dance, or Old-Time Country Dance, etc., is a form of American folk dancing in which the dancers form two parallel lines, alternating male and female. These lines are called sets, and run the length of the dance floor. Couples face across the sets from each other. The sets are then divided into subsets of two couples. The dance consists of a series of moves, or figures, that ends with each couple progressing up or down the set and forming a new subset with another couple. As this is repeated over and over, each couple will dance with every other couple in the set.

The figures vary in difficulty, many being familiar from Square Dancing, and simple circle dances. A caller teaches the dance at a slow walking pace, and then calls the dance itself. Generally, after a few times through the dance, the caller will be heard less and less, and may stop calling altogether.

Contra dances are generally relaxed, family oriented affairs that attract a diverse group of people. The main attraction is the dance itself. Good music is another attraction. A good caller will attract a following as well. Contra dancing is not Country Line Dancing! Contra dancing tends to happen in church halls, auditoriums, schools, and the like. They are generally smoke-free and do not include alcohol consumption. (Having seen drunken individuals try to swing and spin, we can whole heartedly advise against it!)

The only way to really become familiar with Contra Dancing is by going to dances and experiencing them. Chances are, there is a dance not far from where you live. And if there is not, get one going!

III. A Short History of Contra Dance

The modern Contra Dance seems to have evolved from the traditional English Country Dance. References to English Country Dance go back to the 1400's, but the first published edition of dances and tunes comes from John Playford's collection, The English Country Dancing Master, published in 1651. The music from this publication is familiar to performers of Renaissance music, and many recordings of this literature are available. Dances were written to original music, as well as popular music of the time. English Country Dances were usually written to specific tunes, so that in English Country Dance, specific dances are danced to the same tune every time.

Of course, English Country Dance came to the New World with the colonists. And while there was undoubtedly a transatlantic trade in dance books and musical ideas, the early Americans also wrote their own dances and tunes.

The change of name from "Country" to "Contra" dance surely has something to do with the similarity of the two words. However, a French dance book of 1710 was called Recuil de Contredanse, which can be translated as "opposites dance". Hence our term, Contra (opposite) dance.

Country dance was popular in Europe throughout the 18th century, and such composers as Mozart and Beethoven wrote country dance music. By the mid-1800's however, couple dancing was becoming the fashion in Europe. The polka, and then the waltz led to the demise of the Country dance in the cities of Europe. The Country dance tradition was kept alive primarily in the country, and became less fashionable in "sophisticated" society and became more of a folk form. Due to this change in fashion at this time, dancing masters rarely traveled between Europe and America and there was no trade in country dance books. English and American Country dances came to have less and less contact.

By the beginning of the 20th century, English Country dance was essentially dead, while in America, particularly in Appalachia and New England, contra dance and square dancing continued to be a part of people's lives. As with much of America's folk culture, Contra dance gained renewed interest during the folk revival of the 1950's and 1960's. Today there are many dance communities throughout the US, from small local dances to large dance festivals. There has also been a revival of English Country dance both in America and in England.

IV. Putting together a dance band

If there is a contra dance scene in your community, you may want to put together a band and do some playing for it. If you have no dance series, maybe you're interested in getting one going. To put on a successful contra dance you need three things: a band, a caller, and dancers. The purpose of this book is to present ideas and music for a contra dance band.

While there is no absolute standard for instruments or number of players in a contra dance band, the dancers do need to hear two things: a melody, and some rhythm. Melodic instruments could include violin, flute, concertina, mandolin, dulcimer or virtually any other melody instrument. Instruments providing the rhythmic accompaniment include the guitar, piano, hammered dulcimer, and percussion. A dance band could consist of as little as two people, (even a soloist if he or she is really good), or as many as can fit on stage. The only requirement is a clear musical presentation. Too many people can produce a muddy sound, and too few can fall short of the amount of rhythm and energy the dancers need.

Depending on the number of players in your band, and the types of instruments you have at your disposal, a great variety of instrumental combinations can be worked into a dance set. Since these tunes will be played many times over during a typical dance, the band can vary the texture during a tune, and certainly between tunes. While a tune may get played several times by the whole band, an occasional focus on one instrument, such as the violin taking the melody alone, or a combination of instruments, for instance just flute and guitar one time through the melody, will give a tune some nice energy. Certainly when changing from tune to tune, its nice to hear a different texture. All of this will not only give the dancers something to grab onto, but will also give the musicians a creative boost, and in some cases, a much needed rest. Don't forget about percussion. The most common percussion instrument would probably be a bodhran, the drum traditionally used in Irish music. Other possibilities include hand drums of all kinds, Middle Eastern percussion (dumbek, tambourine), spoons or bones, and even washboard. Our band has even been known to have everyone playing on a drum with no melody or chords at all.

Someone in the band should be designated as the leader. This may be a simple process if there is clearly one authority figure who knows the most about the tunes and the dances. However, even in a group of equals, it helps to have one person be the voice of the group. The leader will be the one to communicate with the caller. He or she will be the one to decide on the appropriate set of tunes for a given dance. Depending on the situation, the leader may also be in charge of amplification, the stage layout, band dress, and even payment (you should be so lucky!).

The relationship with the caller is very important. The caller will ultimately decide what dances are being called. The band, or its leader, must be sensitive to the needs of the dancers for particular dances. Some tunes go well with certain dances, and some do not. If the band has a particular favorite set they want to play, good communication is essential so that a good match between dance and tune is made.

V. Instrumentation and Technique

The Hungry Monks usually work as a quintet: violin, mandolin, piano, bass, and guitar. In addition, one or more members of the group will pick up a drum of some sort to add to the rhythm. While the violin and mandolin play almost exclusively melodic lines, the piano has the ability to play either the melody or an accompaniment pattern. The guitar provides the rhythmic foundation and very occasionally plays a melodic line. We also work with a tin whistle/recorder player and a hammered dulcimer player.

Every melody instrument has its own tradition of performance practice that includes tone, articulation, and ornamentation. It is beyond the scope of this book to instruct instrumentalists in tone production (it is assumed that you have a basic musical technique on your instrument), but some ideas on articulation and ornamentation could be helpful.

Articulation

A rhythmic articulation will be helpful for the dancers. A beautiful, sustained legato sound that would be perfect for classical music, might not be appropriate for a dance. The dancers need to hear the basic rhythmic units associated with each type of dance; groups of twos and fours for the reels, and groups of three for the jigs.

Plucked Strings

Plucked strings (guitar, banjo, mandolin) and the hammered dulcimer will obviously have a separate articulation for each note. Basic down/up picking on the plucked strings and the constant hammering of the dulcimer assure that each note gets a solid attack. Attention must still be paid to the basic rhythmic grouping of two's and four's (reels), and three's and six's (jigs).

On the guitar, banjo, or mandolin the down/up picking on a reel is pretty straight forward: there should be a down stroke on the beat and an up stroke on the "and" of each beat.

Red-Haired Boy

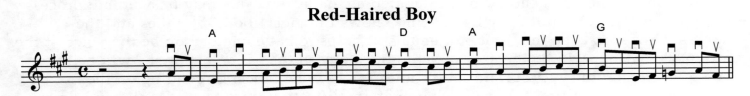

The articulation for jigs can vary depending on the notes in a given measure. You still want the strong beat to be a down stroke, but since there are groups of three notes you generally will not execute a simple down/up pattern as this would result in an up stroke on the second strong beat of the measure (beat 4). Instead, a pattern of down/up/down followed by another down/up/down will ensure that the strong beats (beats 1 and 4) both get strong downbeats. Some players prefer a down/down/up sequence of stokes. As long as the first stroke of each group of three is a down-stroke, this also works. If the notes are in obvious groupings of three's, the following would most likely be the choice of many players:

Kesh Jig

However, depending on the musical line, the player may want to use a straight down/up approach which will have the first group of three beginning on a down stroke, and the second group of three (beats 4,5,&6) beginning on an upbeat:

Water Under the Keel

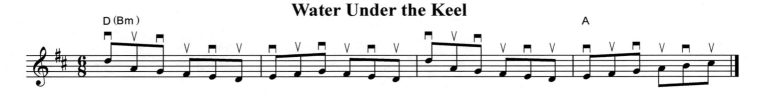

Violin

Emphasizing the rhythmic units on the violin entails attention to the bow. Rather than taking many notes under the same bow, in this style, the violinist will use separate bow strokes for most notes. Called detache, this gives a cleaner articulation to each note and as a result gives a clearer rhythmic articulation to the reel or jig note groupings. Because each note gets a new bow stroke, the violinist should concentrate on the center of the bow where the sound will be more focused and the bow will feel more balanced.

Following are some suggested bowings for reels and jigs. These are by no means the only bowing possibilities, but they do represent a basic foundation for creative bowing possibilities.

The rhythmic grouping of a reel is in two's and four's. A down bow on the the strong beats will give a strong accent to that rhythmic grouping. The most simple bowing possibility would be to take the first two notes of a four note group under one bow and articulate the last two:

Ebenezer

Growling Old Man

Green Willis

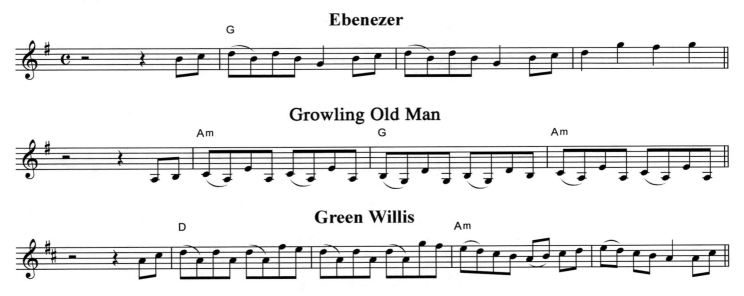

Sometimes, groups of four have three note patterns within them that suggest taking three notes under the bow:

Red-Haired Boy

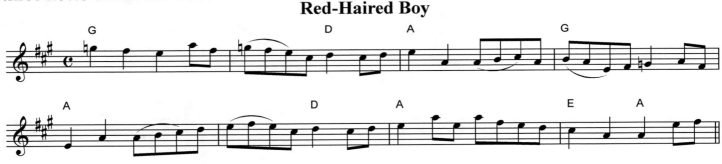

In a jig the rhythmic groupings of three's and sixes should be respected. One basic bowing option is to take a group of three under one bow:

Morrison's Jig

Another idea is to slur the first two notes and articulate the third. Care should be taken to minimize the amount of bow used for the two slurred notes. The amount of bow used for these two notes should equal the amount of bow used for the single, articulated note:

Tobin's Jig

Fasten the Leg on Her

Again, there are many possibilities. Depending on what other instruments are playing, the violinist may decide on bowings, or even change bowings, to suit the situation.

Whistle or Recorder

A whistle or recorder player has the option of how many notes to execute with a single tongue articulation. Once again, with the particular rhythmic grouping in mind, the player may articulate groups of three in a jig:

Tobin's Jig

Or, depending on the intervals between notes, he may choose to tongue one note and then two notes, or two notes and then one. For example, in Water Under the Keel, the jump from the first note, D, to the A and the rest of the line lends itself to a one note, then two note articulation:

Water Under The Keel

At the beginning of Tripping Up the Stairs, the articulation is reversed to two notes and then one:

Tripping Up the Stairs

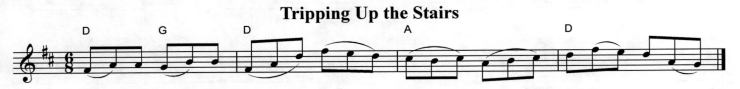

Or he may choose to articulate each individual note if there are lots of consecutively repeated notes such as in Colraine or The Price of My Pig.

Similar possibilities exist for reels as well. The whistle player could articulate three notes and than one:

Mountain Road

Or simply two and two:

Lady of the Lake #2

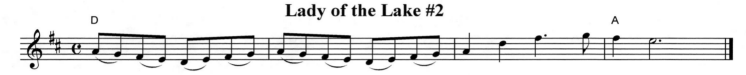

In some cases, four note groupings have groups of three within them:

Dulcimer Reel

Ornamentation

Ornamentation can be an extremely expressive technique that dancers will respond to. Each instrument has its own idiosyncratic ornamental techniques: trills, slides, and grace notes. A violinist will ornament slightly differently than a mandolin player or than a flute player. Once again, the rhythms of the dance need to be heard. Too much ornamentation, while nice in a concert setting, could get in the way at a dance.

Violin

Every instrument has its own unique way of adding to, or taking away from, the melody. Double stops on the fiddle or mandolin, using an open string as a drone while playing the melody notes on an adjacent string can be an effective way of adding variety to the melodic line. Since most of these tunes are in modes that center around notes found on the open strings of the fiddle, its fairly easy to find places to do this. For example:

Dick Gossip's

Becomes

Queen's Polka

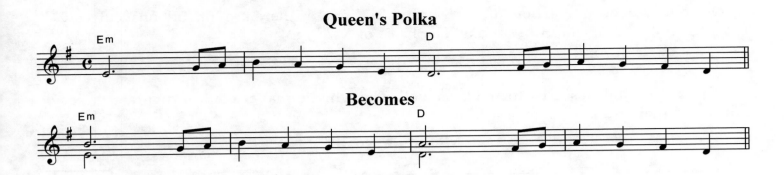

Becomes

Occasionally, you may find that the drone note should be a stopped note as in the second example above. A basic knowledge of chord construction will be valuable in deciding what notes to use as drones. The following is a chart of the basic chords found in most of these tunes. Given a particular chord in a tune, a player could find a drone to play by finding a note in these chords that fits with the fingering of the tune. The note most commonly chosen would be the root or fifth of the chord:

Drone Chord Chart example

Ornaments such as trills or grace notes are an extremely expressive way of spicing up a melody. Trills will usually involve the written note and a note one half step, or a whole step above, depending on the part of the scale you are on. These ornament ideas work for violin and whistle:

Julia Delaney

Becomes

A trill that uses a note a third above the written note can also be effective:

The Road to Lisdoonvarna

Becomes

Whistle or Recorder

The whistle, or recorder, is obviously restricted to one note at a time, but the possibilities for ornamentation are enormous. A simple melodic line can be filled out in a number of ways:

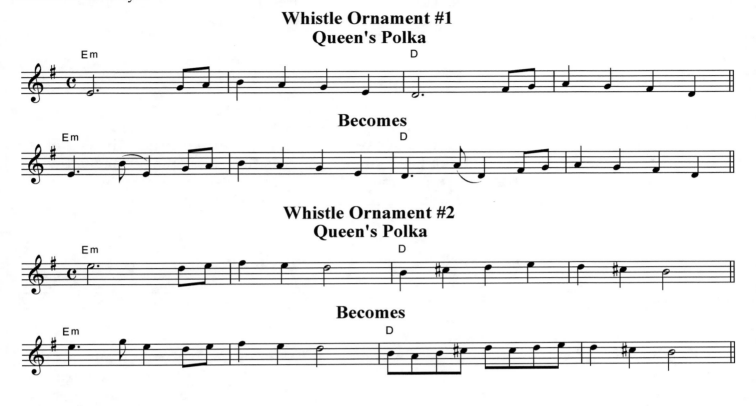

Whistle Ornament #1
Queen's Polka

Becomes

Whistle Ornament #2
Queen's Polka

Becomes

Plucked Strings

Tremolos or subdivisions of the beat on the banjo or mandolin, can breath life into long notes that would otherwise decay on these instruments. For example:

Mandolin ornament example
Queen's Polka

Becomes

Drones also work well on the mandolin or banjo:

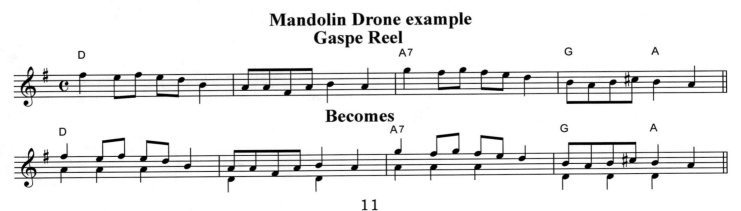

Mandolin Drone example
Gaspe Reel

Becomes

All these factors combine to create and release tension in the music, and hence, in the dance. Tension can be created within a tune by the use of ornamentation and articulation, "shuffle" bowing on the fiddle, "cuttings" (quick tremolos) on the banjo, etc. Tension can be created between tunes by combining them in interesting ways as regards key relationships, and melodic contours. The sets of tunes presented in this book have been assembled with a lot of thought toward tension and release between tunes.

Guitar

The pieces represented in this book fall into two categories of guitar accompaniment playing; Traditional Appalachian or Old-time, and Irish or Celtic style. For American Old-time music such as Staten Island, Magpie or Jaybird the guitar is used primarily as a bass instrument. Instead of filling out large harmonies or chords the guitar player needs to provide a solid and steady bass accompaniment. This is done most commonly by alternating the root of the chord with the fifth or octave root of the chord:

Bass Notes
These work for major or minor chords

The dancers will respond directly to the volume and rhythm that the guitar plays so a steady beat and full sound is vital. It is not always necessary to provide intricate patterns since the dancers have a lot on their minds and are counting on the guitar player to be as rhythmically clear and audible as possible and provide them with what they need to dance successfully. A more experienced player can add bass runs, chromatic bass lines, passing notes and even bass solos to provide variation since each piece will be repeated many times:

Bass Runs

For Old-Time style melodies, standard tuning works well. Once a style or pattern has been set up within a dance you can add rhythmic and/or melodic variety and the dancers will really hear the changes and react to them.

In the Irish, Celtic, and French Canadian pieces such as Tobin's Jig, The Monaghan Jig, and The Kesh Jig, the guitar is a relatively new accompaniment instrument so it has many possibilities in style. One approach is to imitate other instruments like the piano or bagpipes. To imitate the piano the guitarist can use strong staccato strums with moving bass patterns and keep the harmony moving by substituting chords. The implied harmonies on some of the tunes are rather ambiguous. The performer might have to decide whether to play a G major chord or an E minor chord when either could work. More elaborate chord substitutions can be employed. It should be said that this idea of chord substitution is not quite as sophisticated as a jazz musician's idea of chord substitution. We are dealing with triads and seventh chords within a particular key. Extending chords beyond the three note triad and four note seventh chord voicing would be stylistically off the mark. A few tunes in the book have some suggested chord substitutions written in parenthesis. The most common chord substitutions involve relative major and minor chords:

G Major - E Minor - B Minor

D Major - B Minor - F♯ Minor

A Major - F♯ Minor - C♯ Minor

F Major - D Minor - A Minor

Another concept to keep in mind is extending the V (five) chords into V7 chords. Generally, you can determine the key you are in by the letter name of the first chord (the I chord). The V chord would be the chord five letter names from the I chord. For example, the tune Jaybird begins with a D chord. We are in the key of D, and the D chord is the I chord. Counting up five letter names from D (counting D as 1) you find that the V chord is A. You can then extend the A chord to an A7 chord. You can usually extend V chords into V7 chords. Use your ear to guide you. You can only do this with the V chord!

Much of Irish music works very well with a simple drone. A drone is a constant harmony that remains static while the melody flows over the top. Bagpipe players provide this accompaniment for themselves and fiddle players can also drone. A drone is done by playing one chord, root and fifth only, throughout a piece or part of a piece. It is especially fun to use alternate tunings for this so you can strum through all the guitar strings or use damping with the right hand for extra accents. Drop D (DADGBD) or DADGAD are both effective. Some chord shapes are provided here.

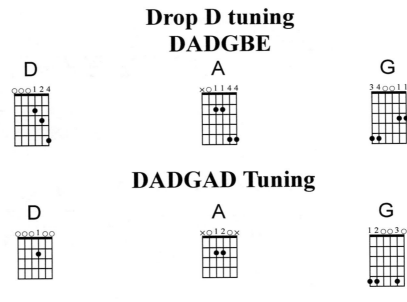

To provide variation and suspense, or tension and release, one could begin a piece with a drone then, after once through, or even after the A section, break into the chord changes.

The dancers might be enjoying the wonderful melody lines, but their bodies directly respond to the rhythm provided by the guitar or piano. The guitarist can build tension by changing volume or a strumming pattern. Good landmarks for accompanists are the "balance and swing" which can be enhanced by strong accents on the balance and a crescendo (soft to loud) dynamic change on the swing. By watching the dancers and experiencing dancing yourself you can begin to add accent to their movements and create an exciting dance experience.

VI. Putting together your own sets of tunes

Traditional fiddle tunes, both American and Irish, are generally constructed with the same amount of measures. Most tunes are divided into two sections, usually called the A and B sections. Each section is 8 measures long and each section is repeated. So, an A section consisting of 8 measures gets repeated, adding up to 16 measures, and the B section gets repeated, adding another 16 measures for a total of 32 measures. Occasionally, a section will only be 4 measures long. In these cases you would play each section twice and the total measure count would be 16 measures (no problem), or you could choose to play each section 4 times to total 32 measures. Four part tunes are fine as is, but 3 part pieces can be a problem. Due to the nature of most dances, which take place "in time" just like the music does, two sections that are 16 measures long give the dancers a familiar sound to steer by. Three part pieces can really screw them up. It is generally acceptable to simply leave off the C section, provided this doesn't present problems melodically. You can get away with a 3 part piece now and then, but you would need to play the piece through a specific number of times to ensure that the dance figure ends at the end of the C section. In other words, a three part piece should be played 2, 4, 6, 8, etc. times to come out even. Pipe On The Hob is a 3 part piece that we play later into the dance if thing's are going well.

In general, sets of tunes keep reels together, or jigs together. It is possible to combine reels and jigs, but the overall pulse must stay the same. Reels are usually in 4/4 time, while jigs are usually in 6/8 time. Either type of tune will work in most cases. Although the time signatures are different, their overall pulse is actually the same. In 4/4 time (Reel time), there are four beats to the bar with beats 1 and 3 getting the strong accent.

Reel Time

In 6/8 time (Jig time), there are six beats to the bar with beats 1 and 4 getting the strong accent.

Jig Time

14

So that while the reels and the jigs have different time signatures, their rhythmic pulse is identical.

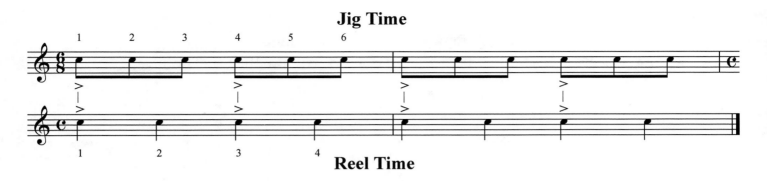

The groupings in this book represent our ideas about key relationships between the tunes. Not only will you appreciate the change of key from piece to piece while playing these sets, but the sense of tension and release that can be created by these key changes is essential to an energetic dance set.

Traditional tunes tend to be played in a limited number of keys, so the possibilities are easily understood. Tunes in major keys tend to be played in G and D. You will also play tunes in A major and occasionally in E major and C major. The minor keys most often heard from are E minor and A minor. You are also likely to find tunes in D minor.

Key relationships like G major and D major, or D major and A major, have a good feel. Since those groupings have logical relationships, they are usually easy fits for key change possibilities. Likewise, A major and E major. Greater tension can be produced by juxtaposing more distantly related keys such as G and A, or D and E. Of course the other part of this equation is the minor key tunes. Mixing major keys and minor keys is another musically interesting device that also propels the dance quite nicely. To generalize a good bit, moving from a major key to a minor key gives the impression of a darkening effect. Because of the nature of most minor tunes, it also helps to deepen the groove bit. Moving from a minor key to a major key brightens things up a lot. This can be an excellent way to relieve the musical tension. Many tunes have A and B sections that change between major and minor. Paying attention to the key relationships between the tunes in our sets can give you lots of ideas about this aspect of putting together dances sets. Substitute other tunes with the same key relationships from the Other Tunes section of the book, or make up new sets using these or other tunes. And of course, there are no hard and fast rules here. Experiment!

The last section of the book gives you some Waltzes. Generally after several contra dances the dancers like to relax with a waltz. The selections we present here were not always intended to be waltzes. We have taken several O'Carolan tunes that were originally in 6/8 or 6/4 time and play them at waltz tempo. As long as there is a feeling of 3/4 time, you can waltz to it. I have also included a couple of original waltz tunes. This is your chance to pull out all the expressive stops. Beautiful tunes played with a rich tone and lots of vibrato will be appreciated here, as long as the waltz rhythm is strong. This is the part of the dance where the band is usually in charge of the length of the dance. If folks are having a good time and enjoying their waltz, keep playing. If everyone is just too tired to move their feet anymore, keep it short and sweet.

VII. The Hungry Monks Tune book

VIII. More Tunes

Reels:

Sugar In The Gourd/Soldier's Joy/The Girl I Left Behind Me

There are other versions of Sugar In The Gourd, but our fiddle player brought this one to us. In a concert setting, we play this one really fast, but we try to control ourselves for dances. Soldier's Joy is a classic that seems to turn up in bluegrass, old time, and Irish settings. We've been known to sing a verse here and there. This set keeps eliminating sharps, so The Girl I Left Behind Me is a great old tune in G.

Hunting The Buffalo/Shove That Pig's Foot A Little Further In The Fire/Billy Church's Memorial Breakdown

A couple of tunes in A surrounding a tune in G. Guitar players usually like to play A tunes with a capo at the second fret, so going from A to G and back again means a little time is needed to deal with the capo. This provides a great opportunity to change the texture at the change of tune.

Over the Waterfall/Flowers of Edinburgh/Congress Reel

While purists of either camp might not agree, we find that the combination of American and Irish (or Scottish) tunes very interesting. Again that key relationship of D major for Over the Waterfall and G major for Flowers of Edinburgh works easily. The transition into A minor for Congress Reel also feels good, with the added surprise of an A major B section on Congress.

Jaybird/Ebenezer/Queen's Polka

One of our all time favorite combinations, these two Old Time tunes and an Irish polka are fun and easy to play. Our whistle player always tries to get some trills in on Jaybird to give it that "bird-like" feel. Ebenezer is one of those tunes that even a beginning guitarist can accompany. More experienced players will find lots of room to fool around. The E minor Queen's Polka always gets the dancers crazy. All three of these tunes are great for the guitarist to play the melody. There is a reason these are called "fiddle tunes": the music fits quite nicely on a fiddle (or mandolin). Guitarists who try to play these tunes quickly find that they are not very "guitaristic". So give your guitarist a chance to shine!

Red-Haired Boy/Gaspe Reel/Return to Milltown

Red-Haired Boy, also known as Little Beggarman, is one of those tunes from Ireland that was taken in by the Americans, and lives happily in both traditions. Gaspe Reel is French Canadian and you can hear right away that it has a slightly different flavor than the Irish or American tunes. The change from D major into D minor with Return to Milltown is wonderful, particularly since the B section of Milltown goes back to D major.

Kitchen Girl/Green Willis/Growling Old Man

Kitchen Girl is a great dance tune that alternates between major and minor tonalities. It also has a great rhythmic kick right at the beginning that can coincide with many dance moves. The change to Green Willis provides some relief from the minor sound of the B section of Kitchen Girl. Growling Old Man should really growl! Another minor/major alternation.

Leather Britches/Temperance Reel/Magpie

Fiddle players seem to love Leather Britches. It's a good tune in G. The Temperance Reel is also in G but with an E minor B section giving that key some releif. Back to straight G major for Magpie. The B section of Magpie has a great rhythmic kick at the beginning that really works with various dance steps.

Tam Lin/Bear Dance

Tam Lin is a really cool Irish tune with a great groove. Written here in D minor, some folks play it in A minor, or even play both versions. Bear Dance is tune we got from an Old Blind Dogs CD. It's one of the easiest B minor tunes available.

Mountain Road/Hunter's Purse/Boyne Hunt

Three Irish tunes. The Mountain Road is a very well known piece. As a bandmate of mine once said, "This tune builds a lot of momentum but never seems to go anywhere". There is some truth to that. The build up of static energy in The Mountain Road is a great thing to experience. The relief comes when the tune changes. The key change into A minor on The Hunter's Purse helps to relieve that static build up, and the change back to D major for Boyne Hunt gives a feeling of return, especially since the tune itself is very similar to Mountain Road (except it does go somewhere!).

Lady's of the Lake/Liberty

Besides being good tunes and fun to play, it's hard to resist playing all three tunes called Lady of the Lake. There is even a specific dance that goes with these tunes. Before we added all three Lady's to the set, we always rounded things out with Liberty. We still keep it at the end to make up a four tune set. Just before my daughter's 8th birthday, she played her first paying gig for the Charleston Contra Dance. She played the bohdran. Nothing fancy, but she has a great sense of time. We figured she would hide out in the back of the band, but the soundman gave her a mic setup and off she went. The band actually consisted of a female fiddle player, a female guitarist/drummer, and my daughter. The band was immediately dubbed "The Lady's of the Lake" by the dancers.

Julia Delany/Dick Gossip's/Paddy Fahey

Julia Delany and Paddy Fahey's are two great tunes in the key of D minor. You find fewer tunes in D minor, but for whatever reason, it's a very soulful key. We break up the minor tunes with Dick Gossip's in D major. In this set it seems that the major tune has the darker feel and builds up tension. Paddy Fahey's has a major B section so the whole set ends in major. My young son has two young friends who often get together and play when the parents are all together. One little girl's name is Julia, and the other is, of course, Delany.

Green Groves of Erin/Man of the House

Two Irish tunes that flow nicely together. Both Green Groves and Man of the House have strong minor licks that every instrument can really dig into. Green Groves seems particularly to be a fiddle showcase. The Donnybrook Legacy won the 2001 Charleston Media Choice Award for "World Music Song of the Year" with our recording of Green Groves of Erin. Go figure!

Juliann Johnson/49 Cats In A Rainbarrel

Forty Nine Cats is a tune our fiddle player brought to us. The B section is very slippery and works well with dances that have either a "hay" or "gypsy" in them. We thought it might be a little tricky to throw this one out at the dancers right off the bat so we put Juliann Johnson in front of it to make sure everyone was on solid footing before we messed around with them.

Little Judique/All The Way To Galway/Reel Eugene

Little Judique is great little tune that ends on the V chord (in this case A major) so it wants to go into something else in D, so we attach it to All The Way To Galway which is a march. Reel Eugene is a great minor tune that ends in major.

Morning Dew/Rakish Paddy/Buttermilk Mary

The first two are traditional Irish tunes. Rakish Paddy is one of those D Mixolydian tunes using a lot of D major and C Major, but where most tunes would begin on the D major, this one actually starts on C major. Buttermilk Mary is a great Bm tune. It's hard but worth the effort.

Nail That Catfish To The Tree/Squirrel Hunters/Squirrel Heads And Gravy

One of those sets that has a thematic element to it, that being dead animals. Nail That Catfish is a good old tune and we couldn't resist putting two squirrel tunes together. Squirrel Heads And Gravy has another life as a hot fiddle tune, but if you can keep your fiddle player under control it's a good one to dance to as well.

Angeline The Baker/Pumpkin Ridge/Rock That Cradle

Clawhammer banjo has been creeping into our instrumentation slowly but surely. Clawhammer players like to play sets of tunes in one key so we did away with keys changes in this set and put together a few of our favorite tunes in D. Angeline The Baker is a standard old tune. We got Pumpkin Ridge from a John Hartford CD. Rock That Cradle is another tune where we might suddenly burst out into singing at any time.

Jigs:

Colraine/The Kerfunken Jig/Scatter the Mud

Colraine is one of those tunes whose A and B sections switch from minor to major, sort of. As in many of these modal tunes, sometimes the performer can make a decision about certain notes being raised or lowered to make a tune sound more minor, or more major. In the A section here, we decided to keep all the G's as natural, giving the piece a feel of E minor. In the B section we use G#'s making all the E chords major rather than minor. Still, the piece ultimately ends in minor and the transition into The Kerfunken Jig has a nice brightening effect, before ending off with another minor tune, Scatter The Mud.

Kesh Jig/Morrison's/Tripping Up the Stairs

The Kesh Jig was one of the first, if not the first, jigs that The Donnybrook Legacy ever played together. A real popular tune that flows right into Morrison's. While many of the

Em tunes have very similar melodies, or licks, Morrison's has a slightly more interesting melodic line that twists and turns a little more than some others. After a nice dark workout on Morrison's, Tripping Up the Stairs relieves the tension while getting a minor tonality started in the B section. Don't forget to play the A section 4 times!

Coppers and Brass/The Pipe on the Hob/The Gander in the Pratie Hole

Coppers and Brass is one of those "can't lose" opening tunes. It has a nice G major sound with melodic figures that lie well on any instrument and predictable chord changes. Pipe on the Hob is a bit more twisted. It's a three part piece so you have to pay attention to how many times you play it. It has a wandering melody and somewhat unpredictable chord changes. We always turn this into a whistle showcase. Gander in the Pratie Hole gets you back into a solid groove.

Road To Lisdoonvarna/Haste to the Wedding/Cliffs of Moher

The Road to Lisdoonvarna is such a pretty tune it could easily be slowed down and played as a waltz. Up to jig tempo it becomes a nice, easy to play, uncomplicated melody that leaves lots of room for the musicians and the dancers. Haste to the Wedding is, by contrast, much busier. The Cliffs of Moher is a classic tune that has a nice rhythmic kick at the B section. The change of tonality from minor to major and back to minor gives this set an interesting feel, putting the darker sounds at the beginning and the end, and having the lighter, major tonality give some relief in the middle.

Tobin's Jig/Monaghan's/Water Under the Keel

This is one of our all time favorite sets! Tobin's Jig and Water Under the Keel are good solid D major tunes that offer several opportunities for interesting chord substitutions. Monaghan's is a lovely, dark, four part tune in E minor. If you really dig into the E minor sound and keep the tension throughout, the change into Water Under the Keel should bring audible sounds of joy from the dancers (maybe the band as well)!

Connaughtman's Rambles/Price of My Pig/Hag At the Spinning Wheel

Another popular session tune, The Connaughtman's Rambles has a nice bouncy feel that is perfect for beginning a dance. The shift to B minor in the B section adds to the interest. Price of My Pig puts us solidly in A minor and is one of those great groove tunes that has a lot of room for improvisation and ornamentation. A word of caution on The Hag at the Spinning Wheel. The B section shifts the accent off the downbeat to beat 4 (counting 6 beats per measure). If all has gone well with the other two tunes and the dancers are really swinging, there should be no problem. However, if the dancers are not completely caught up in the dance, this could throw them off further. From the players point of view, this piece is almost beyond counting. Get the groove and trust it! We got this tune from an obscure CD of collected Irish music. Later we have seen it written as a three part piece, but we always play it as just a two part tune.

The Jaded Optimist/Farewell To Shorty's/Out On The Ocean/Garrett Barry's

I wrote The Jaded Optimist with the specific intention of going from major to minor. My friend Teddy Prause gave me the title. He has a way with words. The Shorty's we are saying farewell to was a gas station/pizza place in Cainhoy, SC where the late, great, all female Bluegrass band called The Marshgrass Momma's used to play. The last two tunes are traditional Irish tunes. I like the idea of putting newly composed tunes together with traditional stuff.

My Darling Asleep/The Swallowtail Jig/Off She Goes

The first tune is just one of the loveliest jigs we play. Swallowtail seems to be the one jig that even old time American fiddlers know. And it sounds great coming out of My Darling. Off She Goes brings us back to the key of D.

Ten O'Clock Jig/Rakes Of Kildare/Gander In The Pratie Hole

The Ten O'Clock Jig is a tune I wrote one lonely evening at about (you guessed it) ten o'clock. The Rakes of Kildare is a tune that our recorder player brought to the band. He's always complaining that these are called "fiddle tunes" for good reason; they lie well on a fiddle and are really hard work for other instruments. So when he said he really liked playing this one, we jumped on it. Gander In The Pratie Hole has a solid groove that ends the set real well.

Up Sligo/The Rollicking Boys Around Tandaragee/Out With The Boys

I learned these tunes from a solo recording by Kevin Burke. E minor tunes always sound good and the rhythmic bounce of Out With The Boys has a nice G major beginning.

Waltzes:

After several contra dances, both the dancers and the band usually cool down a little with a waltz. Not all the dancers will participate in the waltzes. It's a good time for couples who have been separated by the intermingling of people to reconnect and have a slow dance. It's also time for some serious waltzers to show their stuff. For the band it's an opportunity to show how beautifully they can play.

The waltz is always in 3/4 time. It's a dance that has been around for a couple hundred years now. It can be as elegant as a Viennese Strauss ball, or as simple as an attempt to get close to the opposite sex at a high school dance. The best way to understand how to play a waltz is to dance a waltz. Like all dances, the waltz is a function of gravity. You move in a certain way at a certain speed because that is the way it has to be. When astronauts danced on the moon, they had to slow the waltz down considerably to account for the floating effect of the gravity they were experiencing.

This waltz list is a combination of actual waltzes and slow airs that function as waltzes. We particularly like O'Carolan harp tunes with their unusual melodic contour and easy harmonic flow. The possible list of tunes is vast. Anything from classical music, folk, Celtic, and even pop music will work, the only requirement being 3/4 time and the right tempo. The band will only need to play two or three waltzes in an evening, so work up a couple that really fit your sound and dig into them.

I have included a couple of original waltz tunes. I hope you like them. Waltzing With Althea is dedicated to my daughter, who I have been dancing with for many years now. The Four Winds Waltz was written on Orcas Island off the coast of Washington.

Sugar In The Gourd

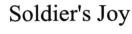

Soldier's Joy

The Girl I Left Behind Me

Hunting The Buffalo

Shove That Pig's Foot a Little Further in the Fire

The Billy Church Memorial Breakdown

Over the Waterfall

Flowers of Edinburgh

The Congress Reel

Jaybird

Ebenezer

Queen's Polka

Red-Haired Boy

Gaspe Reel

Return To Milltown

27

Kitchen Girl

Green Willis

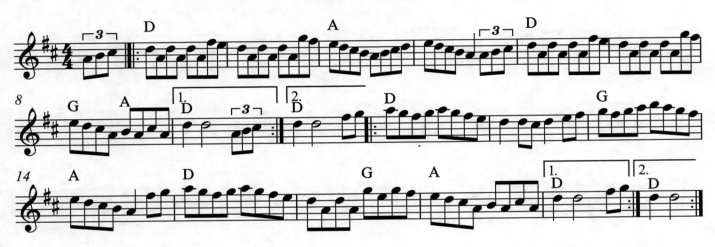

Growling Old Man

Leather Britches

Temperance Reel

Magpie

29

Tam Lin

Bear Dance

Mountain Road

Hunter's Purse

The Boyne Hunt

Lady of the Lake #1

Lady of the Lake #2

Lady of the Lake #3

Liberty

Julia Delaney

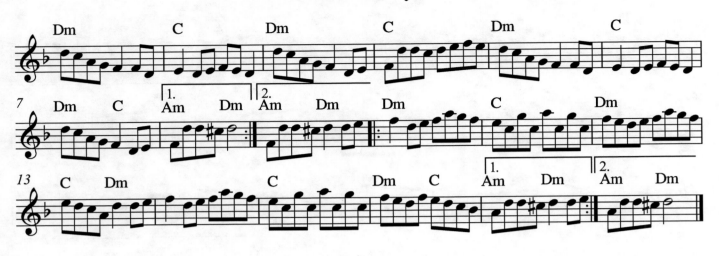

Dick Gossip's

Paddy Fahey's

Green Groves of Erin

The Man of the House

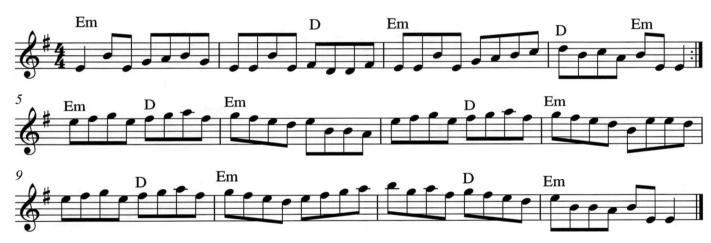

Juliann Johnson

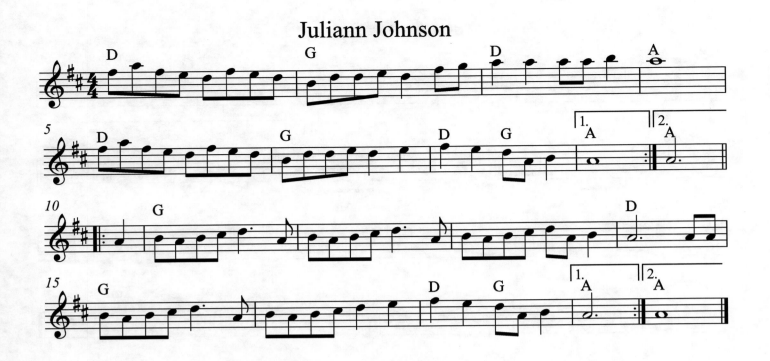

49 Cats In A Rainbarrel

Little Judique

All the Way to Galway

Reel Eugene

Morning Dew

Rakish Paddy

Buttermilk Mary

Nail That Catfish To The Tree

Squirrel Hunters

Squirrel Heads and Gravy

Angeline The Baker

Pumpkin Ridge

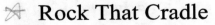 ## Rock That Cradle

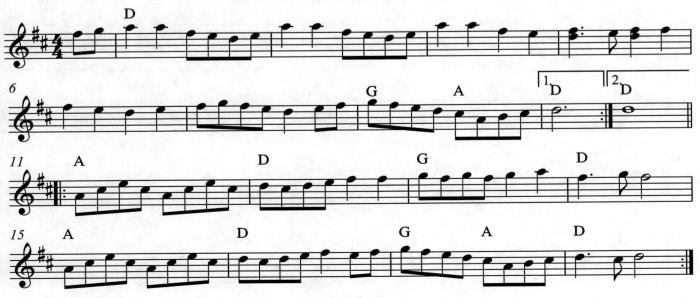

Coleraine

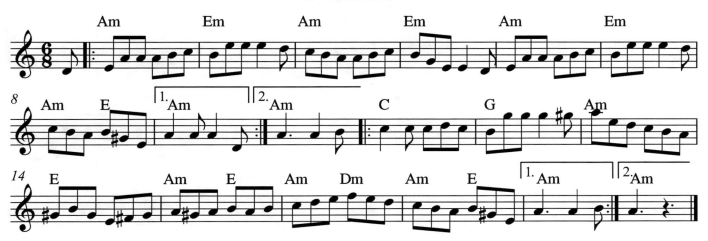

The Kerfunken Jig

Scatter The Mud

Kesh Jig

Morrison's

Tripping Up the Stairs

Coppers and Brass

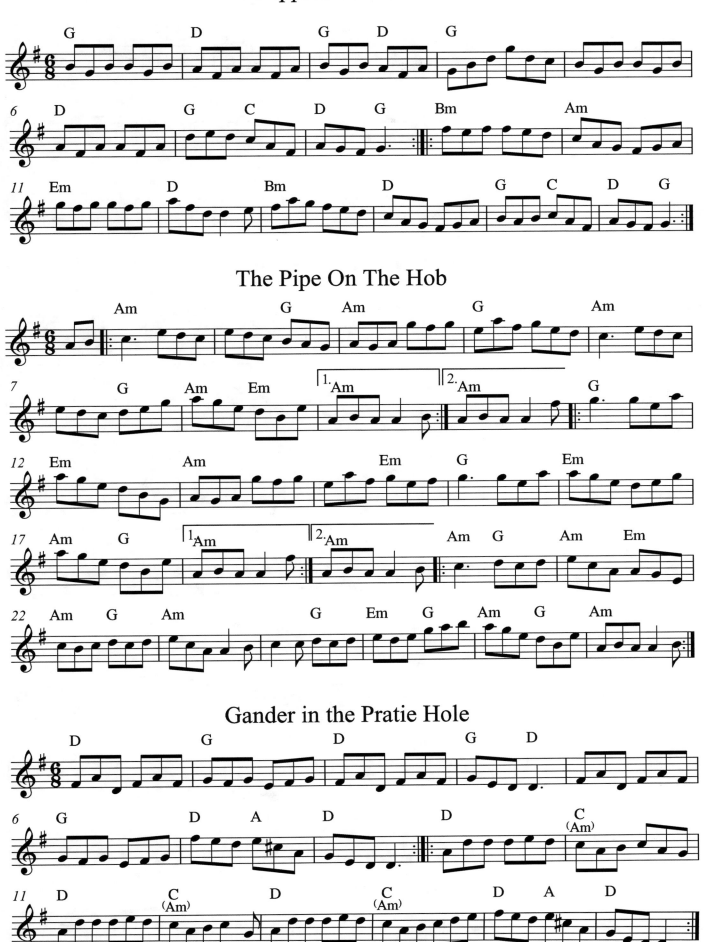

The Pipe On The Hob

Gander in the Pratie Hole

The Road to Lisdoonvarna

Haste To The Wedding

Cliffs of Mohor

Tobin's Jig

The Monaghan Jig

Water Under The Keel

The Connaughtman's Rambles

The Price of My Pig

The Hag at the Spinning Wheel

The Jaded Optimist

Farewell to Shorty's

Out on the Ocean

48

Garrett Barry's

My Darling Asleep

Swallowtail Jig

Off She Goes

Ten O'Clock Jig

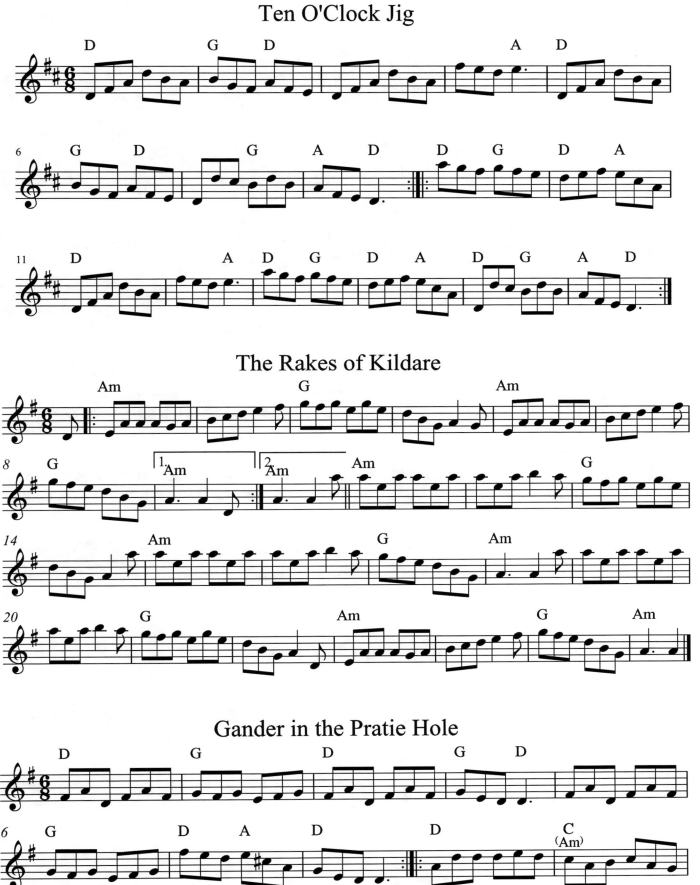

The Rakes of Kildare

Gander in the Pratie Hole

Up Sligo

The Rollicking Boys Around Tandaragee

Out With The Boys

Four Winds Waltz

John Holenko

slow

Hewlett

Turlough O'Carolan

Irish Lamentation

Lord Inchiquin

Turlough O'Carolan

Luke Dillon

Turlough O'Carolan

Midnight On The Water

My Own House

Planxty Irwin

Turlough O'Carolan

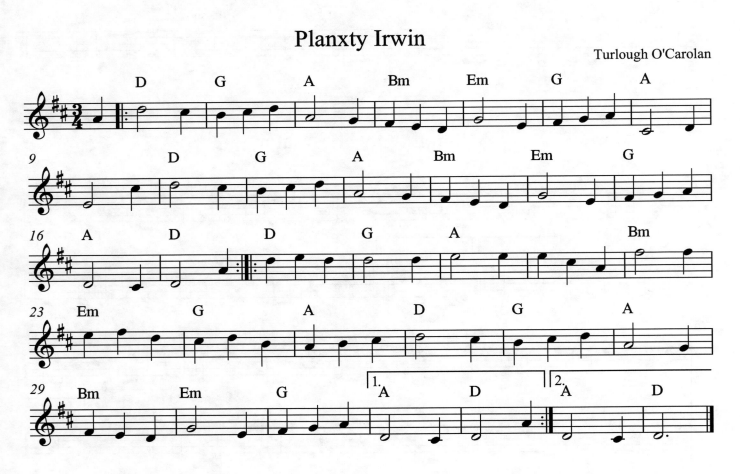

Sheebeg and Sheemore

Turlough O'Carolan

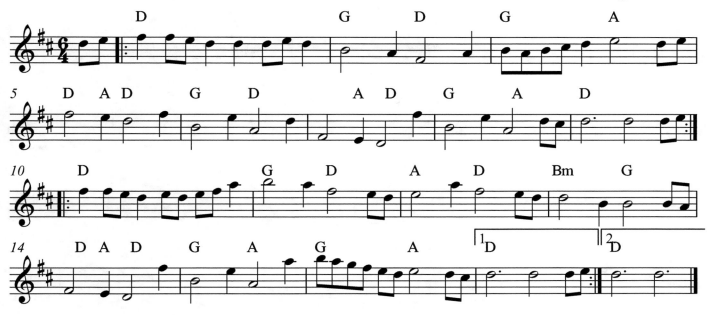

Southwind

Star Of The County Down

Waltzing with Althea

John Holenko

Westphalia Waltz

Arkansas Traveler

Billy In The Lowground

Blackberry Blossom

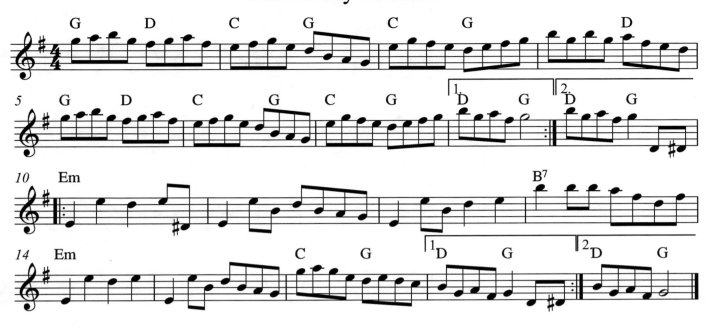

Buttermilk Mary

Cripple Creek

Devil's Dream

Drowsy Maggie

Eighth of January

The Fermoy Lassies

Fisher's Hornpipe

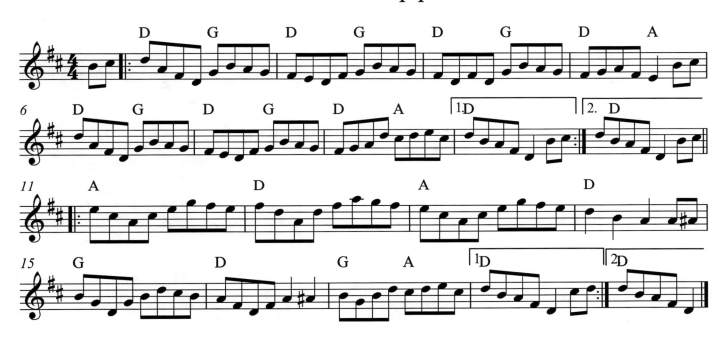

Forked Deer

The Girl I Left Behind Me

Golden Slippers

The Ivy Leaf

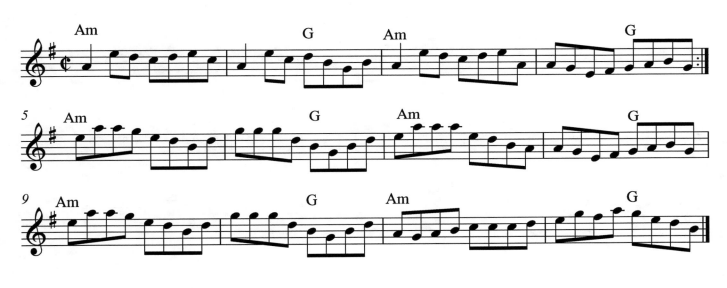

Liza Jane

The Malbay Shuffle

The Mason's Apron

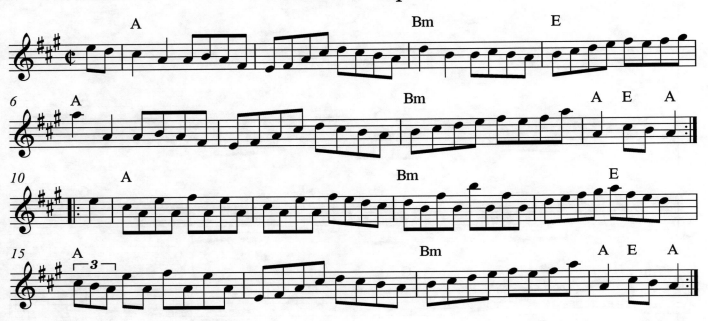

The Merry Blacksmith

Mississippi Sawyer

Nancy Rowland

Petronella

The Poor Scholar

Saint Anne's Reel

The Sailor's Bonnet

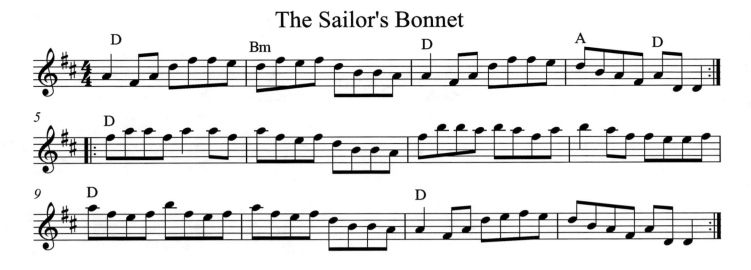

The Ships Are Sailing

Soldier's Joy

Sporting Paddy

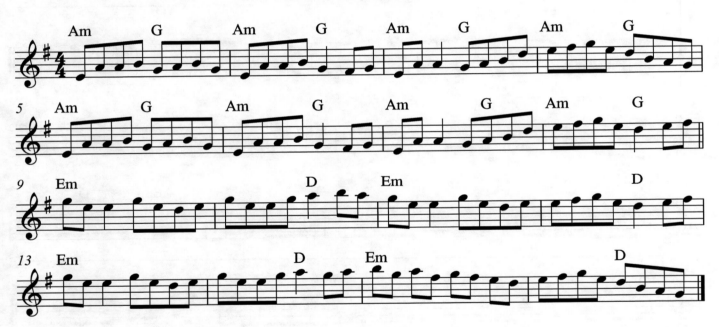

Swinging On A Gate

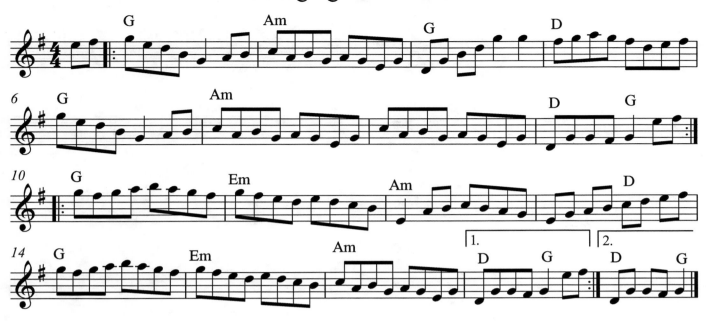

Temperance Reel

Turkey in the Straw

Weave and Way

72

Wedding Reel

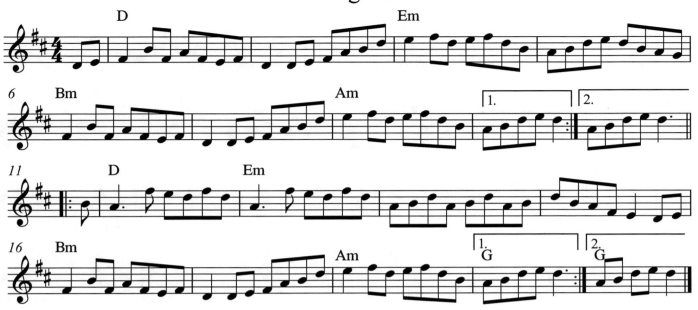

Whiskey Before Breakfast

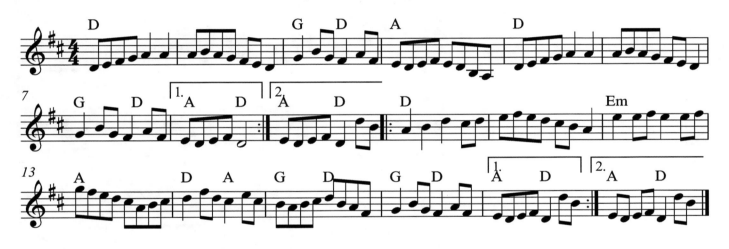

The Wind That Shakes the Barley

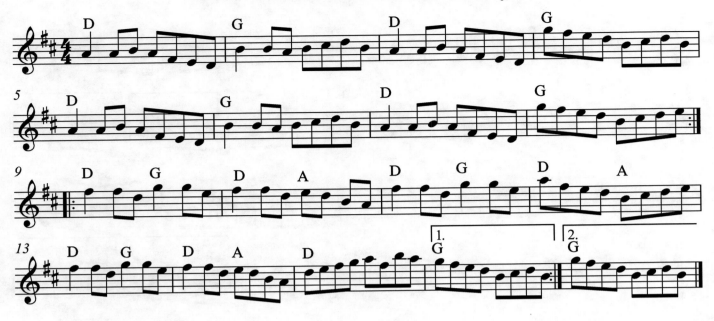

Year of Jubilo

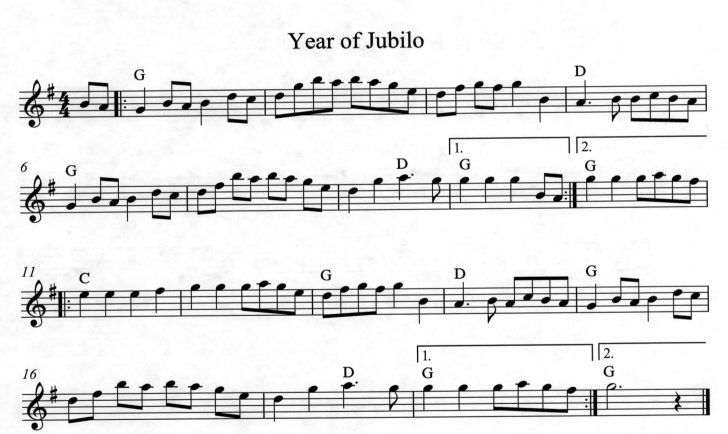

Apples in Winter

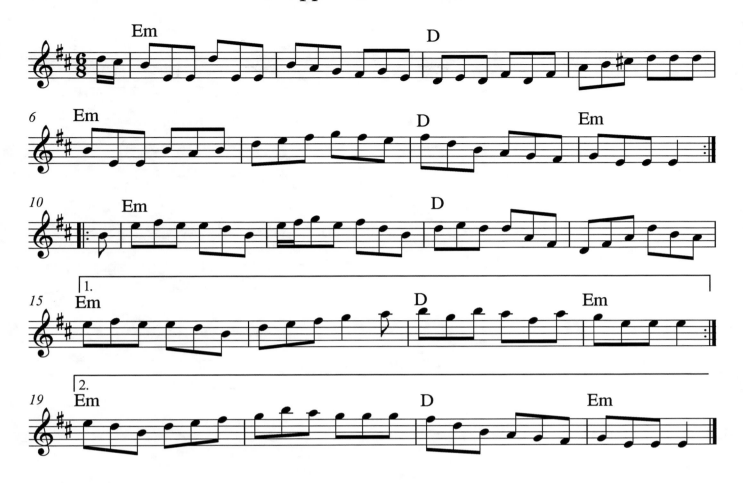

Banish Misfortune

The Frost Is All Over

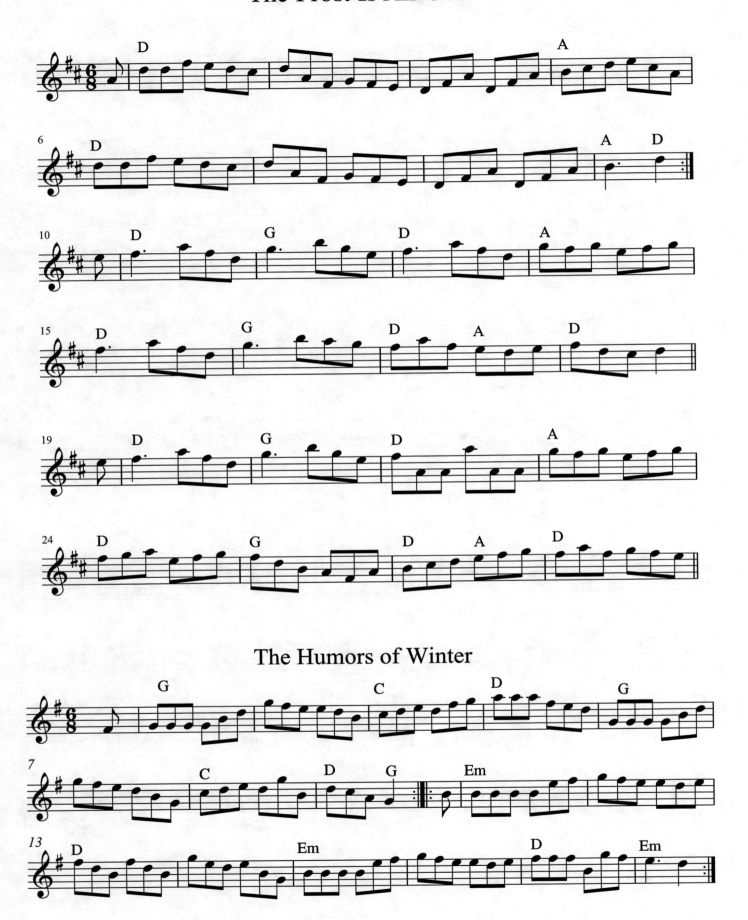

The Humors of Winter

76

The Lark in the Morning

Lannigan's Ball

Off She Goes

Six Penny Money

The Ten Penny Bit

Trip to Killavil

Trip to Sligo

Alphabetical Tune Index